Reasonable
Challenges of Women

Reasonable Challenges of Women

Dr. JoAnn Carroll

To order additional copies of this book, contact:
Xlibris Corporation
1-888-795-4274
www.Xlibris.com
Orders@Xlibris.com
102619

Contents

Dedication

This dedication is to you, women, who are attempting to live your lives with dignity and with purpose by means of the Holy Spirit. The Holy Spirit is your guide for daily living. He is your *"knower"* that is within each of you and he is a richness and great reward in your lives. Within each of you, is the ability to encourage someone along the way, in word or deed.

I pray that as you read the words in this book, that you will benefit greatly and will rise up to meet challenges that were never thought possible, realizing there is greatness on the inside of you.

Introduction

Sometimes women want to operate outside of the box, that is, outside of the box of motherhood, of being a wife, of a grand-mother, or a care-giver. These situations are what is expected of them; they are what they are and women do them. Don't get me wrong, women enjoy giving in every sense of the word, but they are so multifarious or diverse that even women, themselves, don't know all of their strengths, weaknesses, or potential.

But God has so much more for women. If we, as women would just believe and trust in Him, fully, we would realize that God has a special place or places for us as women in this world He created. Even though woman was created after man, we have a special place in the eyes of God. Granted, the woman was never given the orders as notated in Genesis, only the man; yet, God said that everything He created was good and very good, so guess what, that included a woman.

Because of the fall of Adam, each one of us has to pay the consequences for his or her own actions. Disobedience put us out of fellowship with Christ. Adam and Eve were put out of the Garden of Eden because of the sin of disobedience. But God paid the ultimate price for Adam and Eve's sin, the sin of disobedience. God, in the form of Jesus, brought reconciliation to mankind through his suffering and death on the cross. His death, burial, resurrection, and ascension were our path back to the Father, which is in heaven. In other words, He purchased us back from a life of sin, shame, guilt and misery. He paid a debt that He did not owe for mankind and that is why the love of Christ constrains us from doing the things that would utterly destroy us.

I want to talk about some of the challenges that make up the life of a woman. I think you will find the things I share most interesting and very honest.

The Challenges Of Being A Wife

Women, we have to come out of our fairytale mentality that we have developed during our growing up years. Marriage is definitely not a fairytale, it is reality. Let's establish the fact that there are no perfect marriages.

Marriages have to be cultivated and it should be God-Christ centered in order to function properly. Women have to learn how to be wives and men have to learn how to be husbands. Husbands and wives have to learn each other, their likes and dislikes, habits, personalities, etc. Only Christ can establish a marital relationship that functions effectively and lovingly. Marriage is beautiful or it can be beautiful and successful but only through Christ. He is the only one that can smooth out the rough edges. The bible is our greatest resource and guide into what a wife's role really is. So, I urge you to become a Christ-centered woman.

Next, I would like to address the loss of a spouse. We all know that eventually there is the loss of a spouse through the inevitable circumstance called death.

The Loss Of A Spouse

When a spouse passes away, what is the focus after the initial shock? The first thing is to take care of the business at hand. Everything is now on your shoulders. There is no time to grieve right away. You are numb but still have to function and handle the business affairs in preparation for the actual burial services. After mechanically handling the immediate business and getting through the burial services, then you have the luxury of grieving. So far, you have been operating mechanically with a feeling of numbness and disbelief in some cases, especially if the death was sudden or unexpected. The grieving process has to take its course, but don't stay in that place too long; it is not good.

After the grieving process, comes the thought of "what do I do now". What is the next step? At first, you feel a sense of loss and if that is not enough you feel lost as well, sometimes afraid, and you can't pull your thoughts together as well as you would like.

You know what it means to be single after all you were single before; however, after married life your entire mindset or focus is so different.

Therefore, becoming single again, after marriage is a very different and very challenging experience. The difference is that you have come together and worked closely and deliberately with an individual to build a lasting relationship. You have bonded with another individual. You have become one with your soul mate.

And anything or anyone that was once bonded and is now torn apart are never the same whatever the separation, but one must move on. The next steps are to get your finances generating and gain some type of momentum for your life. In this role, new ideas form, you learn to be self sufficient; you learn to make decisions that affect your life in a positive way. Wisdom has to make her entrance and remain to be able to go on.

It is very necessary and important at this point to find new interests and draw closer to God at the same time.

Develop new friendships; join a Christian women's group or some type of positive women's group. It is important to grow in grace and love yourself through all of this and really find out who you are as a person. If you have children, love and embrace them and allow them to embrace you. You must feed off of each other and gain strength from one another and grow together and figure out what is best for everyone involved. I'm not saying you have all the correct answers that you would desire, however, you are moving and operating in what you know, trusting you are moving in the right direction for your life/lives. Let's discuss factors that affect a woman after the death of her spouse and becoming a single parent.

The Challenges Of Widowhood

The loss of a spouse and being left alone to rear children can sometimes create a bitter taste and an uncertainty in a woman's life. If fear becomes a factor, it causes the woman to feel vulnerable. She can find herself functioning in a negative vein because of insecurity and fear.

She can become frightened and unsure about the future. I choose to believe that a widow left with children will love and cherish and nurture her children and try to diminish her children's fears and uncertainty. She must be strong, however, and learn to stand confident that God will see her through. Her children need to feel protected and safe. She can't be given to panic or despair because this will distort her logic and her ability to use sound judgment. Without sound judgment, everyone she is responsible for will suffer needless and negative consequences.

If this widow stays Christ-centered, she will gain the strength that she needs to survive and also her children will gain strength and courage for day-to-day living. Sometimes, a woman goes through a time of transition in her life while she is still trying to regain her footing and in this society she needs to regain her footing, quickly.

Challenges Of Motherhood

Motherhood is a unique experience. Motherhood is also what you make it—good, bad, or indifferent, successful or unsuccessful. Successful parenting depends on how we as women think, how we view parenting, or what our parenting styles represent.

Our positive, negative, or indifferent attitudes are factors, because our attitudes play such a vital role in shaping our vision, our desires, our dreams, our goals, and will inevitably shape our outlook on life and the lives of the children in our care.

As mothers, we are called upon to perform multiple and countless tasks at any given moment. We have to be available and able to respond at all times.

A major role as a mother is that of a teacher. We teach in every sense of the word. Whether we teach with words or teach with actions, nevertheless, we are teaching.

Let's talk about the life of an infant for a moment. When your infant snuggles close to you, is your touch gentle and loving, mothers? Does this innocent life that has been loaned to you for a season, know the love in your eyes or the gentle caress of your touch as you care for them? Do they know gentle hands when they are being fed? If they become ill, can they count on you to be there for comfort? The role of a mother is care-giver, nurse, chauffeur, teacher, counselor, and the list goes on. We become whatever we need to be and we cherish those moments.

I have found that being a mother has great rewards. It's like an exquisite painting of great value or it's like creating a great masterpiece of some kind and reaping the rewards of how it turns out.

As infants grow into toddlers, they tend to explore their surroundings. When they fall down, are you there to pick them up, dust them off, and tell them that it's okay? Do you know the magic of kissing the hurt and making it better? It's something to think about, isn't it?

When a child becomes school-age and priorities change, they are no longer toddlers, but they are beginning to think for themselves. The baby days are gone. They are more self-sufficient and are forming their own ideas for themselves. This sounds good, doesn't it or does it? At this stage in life, they should be guided through the challenges that lie ahead. They will encounter different personalities in school, so, hopefully they have learned some survival skills.

They must learn the art of sharing at school and at home. From first to sixth grades, this developmental stage of activities is the key to a balanced life of growing and being exposed to the world and life issues. Our parenting skills will take our children a long way if we, as mothers, have given them the tools and the know-how that was necessary for development and if we have nurtured and empowered them in the correct manner for life's challenges.

Prayerfully, we as parents and mothers have learned these important skills ourselves in order to instruct our children in their developmental stages of life and have surrounded them with healthy environments.

As middle-schoolers, what they have learned by this time is already a part of their character. In most cases, what they have been exposed to begins to manifest in their behavior. I reiterate, in most cases. Sometimes other behaviors appear that are foreign to the mother. However, the behaviors should still be manageable. In this place, decision-making will play a huge role in every area of their lives. Middle-schoolers are becoming their own person and this is displayed differently in each child.

Another level of growth is high school and high school presents its own challenges and motivators. Strong adult opinions are being offered almost on a daily basis from the high-schooler. A resistance to authority sometimes takes place while trying to find a balance. They are preparing for life on their own and that preparation can be extremely challenging for a parent, especially if that parent still sees a high-schooler as their "baby".

Mothers have to allow them space to mature and that is an uncomfortable position for a mother because you want to ensure they are making the right decisions. Hopefully the efforts and the hours of training that we as mothers worked so diligently to instill in our children has been instilled and has become an integral part of their being and their development. In this place we know that if they make themselves proud, they will also make us as parents proud. Motherhood is quite challenging because the role is so unique, but the rewards are endless.

As a result of hard work and consistency we as mothers can sit back and breathe a sigh of relief and know that everything is alright.

Next I would like to address a different kind of woman. A woman that is driven by strong passion can suddenly erupt with a strong outburst of emotion. This woman is called the stormy woman.

The Stormy Woman

Storm/stormy = an atmospheric disturbance characterized by a strong wind; a strong outburst of emotion, passion, excitement; to be violently angry.

Have you ever seen someone where their very demeanor was that of anger? It seemed they were angry with the world and that life had given them such a terrific blow it was very difficult for them to let go or move forward. When mainly all that needed to happen was for them to forgive, get counseling, refocus, and let the past go. Would that be an easy thing to do? The answer is absolutely not.

But to be willing to work through everything with the purpose of being set free from the bondage that holds the mind, the will, and the emotions in captivity is crucial at this point. Therefore, giving yourself permission for growth to take place in your life would be so rewarding.

The stormy woman only harms herself, especially is she chooses to hold on to the past. She keeps everyone around her at arm's length or at a great distance and won't allow anyone to get close to her, therefore leading a lonely and unproductive life and blaming others for her misfortune. She is afraid to let go and the underlying cause is fear and insecurity.

A person cannot go any further than their ability to forgive, to understand what happened or what didn't happen and be willing to keep moving forward in life in a healthy fashion. An individual cannot move any further than their ability or willingness to forgive. A stormy woman is a dangerous woman, in that she has almost no limits as to what she will do at any given point. She is out of control. There are no boundaries. For the stormy woman her very insides are raging. She has very few friends or no friends. She runs everyone away that tries to befriend her.

Because of her own insecurities and failures she is very untrusting. She sees the world in a negative light instead of a positive light. In fact, her world is a world of darkness. There is doom and gloom all around this woman and something must be done, but what? How do you get this stormy woman to be happy and to find contentment in life? How is she to be delivered out of this fog?

What is the key to her deliverance? Is there no hope? The answer to this question is yes there is hope. This woman has to know that she needs help and she has to reach for it. Reach out to God and receive direction in this matter.

This stormy woman has to change her focus and examine her life and her lifestyle to find out if things can be done differently. She needs to earnestly work at changing her mindset, transforming her negative thoughts into positive ones. To transform the mind means to renew the mind. You may be wondering how she can renew her mind, a mind that is so confused. She can renew her mind by becoming Christ centered. She can allow Christ to be her guide and her counselor.

She has to allow Him to lead her in paths that are good for her—paths that cause her to have good success. Who wouldn't want that? However, this will be a process. She did not get in the state she's in overnight; it was a process.

She will have to go through a process to change her prospective but it will be worth it in the end. She will be excited with the outcome.

Cruelty Of Life Issues

Naomi, in the book of Ruth, grew very bitter and angry because of the hand she had been dealt by losing her husband and her two sons. She was in a foreign land because of the famine in her native land. But her daughter-in-law, Ruth, helped her to see and understand that she was not alone. Ruth decided to return with Naomi to her native land of Judah because Naomi had nothing left for her in Moab. She needed to try and regain some of what she had lost even though she was not too hopeful. Of course, when Naomi returned to Judah she did not return the same as when she left. Naomi had become very bitter, indeed. Her experiences had changed her perspective on life. Cruelty of life issues had developed for Naomi.

Women have to realize that they are not alone. Stop, women, and think about where you are in life and think about where you want to go. You can always dream. Never lose your ability to dream because if the dream ever fades, so does your willingness to get up and try again.

Hopelessness is not pretty. Eventually, Naomi returned home and took her daughter-in-law, Ruth, with her and found wealth, prosperity, and happiness. She found more than she thought possible. She found more when she returned than what she had when she first left home. What if Naomi had dared to dream? What if she had refused to get up and try again? What if she had allowed despair to cripple her thinking? But she dared to dream and it paid off more than she ever imagined. So don't give up women, don't throw in the towel and say what's the use. Remember there is always hope as long as you are willing to get up and try one more time.

So, it was worth going back home for Naomi even though she was bitter when she went; but in time she reaped the good of the land. The same for you, it will be worth every effort to go where there is prosperity and happiness even if it means returning to a hometown or city that you left never expecting to return to it again.

You never know what good things God has in store for you through your obedience and by putting your trust in Him. I like to say that God is just good like that. For Naomi it was a challenge of the heart.

Challenges Of The Heart

The **heart** = the hollow, muscular organ in a vertebrate animal that receives blood from the veins and pumps it through the arteries by alternate dilation and contraction.

A dictionary definition of the **heart** says—our inmost thoughts and feelings and our source of emotions.

What is my heart saying? Where is my heart leading me? Challenges of the heart are not always romantically linked, although there is nothing wrong with it.

There are various challenges of the heart that I would like to tap into:

- Again what is my heart saying?

- My heart could be telling me to go back to school.
- My heart could be telling me to change careers.
- My heart could be telling me to adopt a child.
- My heart could be telling me to purchase a home.
- My heart could be telling me to write a book.
- My heart could be telling me to help someone in college.
- My heart could be leading me to share my testimony of life's experiences.
- My heart could be leading me to share my faith with others.
- My heart could be telling me to become healthy.
- My heart could be telling me to eat nutritious foods.
- My heart could be telling me to exercise and tone my body.
- My heart could be telling me to be a little more friendly or helpful.
- My heart could be telling me to smile more.
- My heart could be telling me to let go of some old traditions and to get some new or fresh ideas.
- My heart could be telling me to become a mentor.

The question is whether I would be willing to share what my heart is saying with someone else. If not, why not? It is a precious thing to be led by the heart as well as by the Spirit of God as long as it is the proper thing to do and it is the right thing to do. Also as long as it will benefit someone and not destroy them or their dreams. The heart has to be full of love and compassion, yet disciplined and godly in nature. Proverbs 4:23 declares, "Guard your heart above all else, for it determines the course of your life." If your heart gives you a desire for a mate or companion I pray that the two hearts will mesh and a lasting relationship will emerge saturated with the energy and love of Almighty God and that your thoughts and ambitions will energize you and give you success in your endeavors.

Don't be surprised at what your heart may require of you. Hearts are tender and pliable so treat your heart with care. If your heart has been hardened by life's challenges, by all means allow Christ to soften your heart through His word.

Allow His love to melt away the ugly stuff and allow the love to replace all of the pain and disappointment of your past that has been trapped within your heart and allow the Holy Spirit to take root and filter through every crevice of your being, and give yourself permission to accept the love that was intended in the first place. You'll be glad you did. Now let's explore the actions of the ambitious woman.

The Ambitious Woman

The ambitious woman is a woman that is unstoppable in her creativity and in her actions. She acts upon the creative thoughts that enter her mind. She sees that as an opportunity to move forward and experience something she has never experienced before, in other words, she seizes the moment. An ambitious woman loves to explore. She loves to explore new avenues or new business ventures or new territories with the possibility of renewed passion for herself as well as earning extra revenue for herself.

She is not selfish; she will share her ideas with those of like interest, such as friends or those who share in her excitement about her future. This woman is moved by unexplored territories and untapped resources that will enable her to accomplish her dream.

Her excitement is contagious and always filled with delight with the prospect of new and different possibilities. She wasn't always like this. She started out with just a dream or a goal to accomplish one idea and an excitement grew within her after the dream became a reality. This spurred her on to attempt something beyond what she thought was even possible or imaginable. She was in awe of the endless possibilities of how far personal visions and dreams could take you if you believed; so please believe in yourselves.

The ambitious woman is full of adventure. She is not afraid to step out and try what she has never tried before; even if she has already attempted a venture of some kind prior. She starts to think of how she can do something better. In the meantime, she is constantly thinking of new and innovative ideas and her creativity is running rampant with different ways to express her talents and expertise. She is inspired by everything around her. Her mind tells her she could become an entrepreneur, an artist, or an international sensation.

Spiritual consciousness or awareness is motivating her daily to achieve as much as she can for the purpose of sharing with others her expertise and wisdom, which in turn will cause other people she comes in contact with to become motivated and move forward with their dreams, their visions and their goals. She ignites an excitement that is difficult for anyone to smother. When she speaks, everyone listens because she has proven that all you need is vision and motivation to get started.

The ambitious woman will go far in life because she has the courage to move forward without reservation to ensure that her goals and dreams will materialize and that they will become a reality. Even if at first she fails in her attempts and endeavors, she is not afraid to try again. The old adages, if at first you don't succeed, try again. She is not easily swayed or influenced to give up. She is not easily discouraged because she can see the finish line. She can see the light at the end of the tunnel and she believes in what she is doing. The ambitious woman believes that the work she is doing is worthwhile and that it will come to fruition, her mind tells her it will work.

Faith—she has faith in what she has set out to accomplish. She cannot be convinced otherwise. An ambitious woman is positive in her approach and has strong convictions about life and it shows. She surrounds herself with those who share the same visions and dreams, people that envision them accomplishing their goals, their desires and their dreams. Their drive and their ambition are to succeed in whatever they set their minds to deliver. These ambitious women are unstoppable. Come on, get up and get going. You will be amazed at your abilities and how far they will take you if you try. So try.

At this point in the book we realize that in anything there are major challenges and minor challenges. Let's delve into some of these, shall we.

Minor Challenges Versus Major Challenges

A minor challenge is one that has a lesser degree of importance, however never negating the fact that it is a challenge. A minor challenge may include anything from learning that a class necessary for a college course is not being offered this semester, but it is being offered the following semester; also it could entail not getting first place in a poetry contest, but you placed second or third; a minor challenge could include going to a sale at the supermarket and the food item you wanted was sold out, or being an athlete and not doing as well as you would have liked and the prize that you coveted escaped you. These are not life threatening by any stretch of the imagination, just disappointing. Again, I am not negating the fact that these are challenges. There are so many minor challenges that I cannot name them all; however, I think you get my point.

Here are some of the major challenges that one can experience; Graduating from a university of your choosing and not being able to find a job in your selected field of study; especially if the field took years of study; A job promotion that did not materialize after being promised. This would be a major challenge. A couple getting married and finding out later that they are unable to have a child; death of a spouse or child; having to suddenly be a care giver for an ailing parent or spouse. A major illness that has materialized and no one saw it coming. All of these are major challenges and there are so many more.

The positive sides to major challenges are: years of study at a college or university and finally you have the opportunity to take on what you have always wanted to do in life; or the position that you were waiting for finally came through. You can finally afford the house or car that you dreamed of owning. You have wanted to retire and travel abroad and the time has finally arrived, etc . . . shall I go on or do you have the picture? I believe you have the picture.

Life itself is a challenge however; challenges are what we make of them. What I mean by this is in order to come out with positive influence in any challenge depends on how it is viewed. All challenges are tests. Each detour in life stretches our focus and creativity. Will we have to refocus in order to finish what we started?

What will be considered minor and what will be considered major? It is all up to the individual as to how or what the response should be. Realistically speaking, some situations are major, but are we as human beings looking at things as though they are major when in reality they are really minor? Are there stress factors that should not be present as one deciphers the importance of a situation?

How about taking the time and slow things down a bit in order to assess situations calmly, and with a great deal of care and rationale in order to make the right decisions.

Proverbs 3:5-6 says, "Trust in the lord with all your heart; do not depend on your own understanding. Seek His will in all you do, and He will show you which path to take."

There will always be challenges. Will we overcome challenges or will we allow them to overtake us and keep us from our destiny and purpose? Life moves on, so don't ever stop growing and anticipating great and mighty things to occur in your life and don't allow yourself to get bogged down in the "what if's" of life. "What if's" as a rule, never materialize, so go with reality or just go another way, go with the things that are actually happening and allow yourself to work through them in a way that will speak volumes later. Have an expectancy of the success that you are working toward on an everyday basis and remember you are a winner. Let's now discuss the winner in you.

The Winner

Women we are winners. Our very lives depict success in every area of our lives. Women work at contributing to society on a daily basis, starting in the home and then moving or shifting outside of the security of home. You may ask how we contribute to society. My answer to that is very simple. Women rear their children to be good citizens in the world, to be honest, to have a good self-image, and to be diligent in their studies in school and rise to challenges which can strengthen their character. This in turn teaches children, youth, and young adults to have self confidence and to know their worth.

Women/mothers develop into the gracious people God intended for them when He breathed the breath of life into them. Women, we are okay, never doubt that. We have so much to offer. We have tons of creativity inside of us and so many brilliant ideas that haven't even been tapped into yet. Kindness is a woman's greatest quality along with being a comfort to many in diverse situations. Women of grace, let's continue to distribute love, joy, and a presence of God's peace to whomever we come in contact with during our journey here on earth as part of our reasonable service to God.

Let's exhibit hope for a dying world and women let's go through our challenges as smoothly as possible so we can be there for the next generation of women that will need our expertise, our creativity, our peace, our excitement, our gifts and our abilities that only we possess. God has given women his best so let's use what we have been entrusted with because remember we are winners in every sense of the word.

Conclusion

In our everyday walk we are faced with many seemingly insurmountable obstacles. However, we know that nothing is too difficult for God to see us through and we know that we can and will be everything that God has ordained for us to be. We, as women, accept the challenge and step up to the plate and never let our guard down or drop the ball on our vision and dreams here on earth.

Women of God don't fret for He never leaves us alone. We always have the presence or the Spirit of God to guide us and walk along side of us to give us the tip of the day, which is to "be encouraged and of good cheer, He says I have overcome the world". For us, that means we can achieve our goals and live out our dreams. Whatever is in our hearts that is worthwhile and good we can accomplish with pride. Set your hearts in great wonder as women of promise. Don't allow anything to deter you from your journey and field of dreams and visions that are inside of you. Those dreams and visions are there for a reason and for a purpose.

Women, you have much to offer, so gird up your minds and hearts and forge ahead. Let's move forward and push back those negative thoughts of "I can't", because "yes you can". Push back negative, bad, or ugly things that might have been spoken over you at some point in your life and know that God is saying something different. He (God) says that we are fearfully and wonderfully made and there is nothing we can't do with His help and guidance.

Get those positive thoughts, those beautiful thoughts into your mind and let's run with that. You are special and that's why we were made special. We were made for endurance and were given a type of strength that can only come from God. Women were given great character and that is why the evil one has tried to block or shatter or tear down the self-esteem of women all over the world.

We were given a type of strength where, at times, it is difficult even for us as women to understand because it is so powerful. But it was given in order for us as women to stay afloat of situations and conflicts and things that would tend to try and pull us down. We can stand women. We can do it.

We have the where-withal to stand. Let's agree together to stand. We are more than conquerors, don't you realize that? Who told you that you couldn't stand? Don't believe the lies of the evil one. Women you are beautiful because God chose to make you beautiful.

God has blessed women with inner beauty so look inside yourselves and see the real you, your real inner beauty. Pull it up and out and develop it—it has always been there. You just didn't know it was there, therefore you didn't know how to find it or if you found it you didn't know what to do with it. But aren't you glad it's there? I'm speaking of that inner beauty that cannot be taken away from you unless you allow it to be. Even then it wouldn't have been taken away—you would have given it away. So women, hang on to your inner beauty and don't let it escape.

Women, we are beautiful not only to ourselves but also in God's eyes. We are gorgeous creatures that He created and declared that everything He made was good and very good. Guess what women, the good and very good is speaking of mankind and that means you. Why do you think there is such a spiritual fight, such warfare sometimes where women are concerned? It's because we are so special and have so much to offer and the enemy of our souls doesn't want it to manifest, so we become confused as to our identity and don't know what to do with ourselves. But Christ is here to straighten everything out in our lives and to make us whole. Women don't you want to be made "whole"?

Women, know that you are teachable, smart, and wise and you possess such a dignity that it makes you such a threat, in a positive way, to society. Women, you are incredible so don't forget who you are and please allow yourselves to believe in who you are as women. After all, you are that incredible woman of purpose and that incredible woman of destiny and your future is looking awfully bright to me.

Bibliography

New Living Translation, Second Edition, copyright © 2007 by Tyndale House Publications, Inc., Carol Stream, IL, Proverbs 3: 5-6.

The NIV/KJV Parallel Bible, copyright © 1985 by Zondervan Bible Publisher, Grand Rapids, MI, Genesis 1:31.

Webster's New World Dictionary of the American Language, Second College Edition, copyright © 1972, Guralnik, David B. Editor in Chief, The World Publishing Company, New York and Cleveland, heart, storm, stormy.